TAKE A RIDE with MICKEY

By **SEYMOUR REIT**

Illustrated by **GUELL**

Disney PRESS

NEW YORK

1 3 5 7 9 10 8 6 4 2

Library of Congress Catalog Card Number: 91-71336
ISBN 1-56282-060-5

Mickey and his friends are off to see the world. With a rush and a roar, their jet plane rises into the air.

"Flying is fun!" says Minnie. "How do you think we'll travel around in the countries we visit?"

"There must be *lots* of fun ways to get around," says Mickey. "Let's see how many we can try!"

In London, England, Mickey and Minnie board a double-decker bus and climb to the top.

"I'm glad we're sitting up here," says Minnie. "Look at how much we can see."

"You're right!" says Mickey. "I can even see a nice place to have tea!"

A team of reindeer pull Mickey and his friends in a sleigh across the snow-covered ground in Finland.

"This is the best way to get around in the winter-time," says Daisy.

Donald laughs. "Yes," he says. "Everyone travels like Santa Claus here!"

High up in the mountains of Switzerland, Mickey,
Minnie, Donald, and Daisy ride in a cable car. The
car glides along on extra-strong cables that are
supported by tall steel beams.

"There's Goofy!" says Donald. "He's riding the cogwheel train."

"Look at the train's big wheel," says Daisy. "It has teeth that fit into the grooves on the track and help pull the train up the steep hill."

Donald and Daisy take a gondola ride in Venice, Italy, while Mickey, Minnie, and Goofy wave to them from a water bus. Venice has no roads and no cars, but there are canals and boats everywhere.

"Let's take a water taxi to the train station when we leave," says Minnie.

"Okay," says Mickey.

"Do you think they ever have traffic jams here?" Goofy asks.

Surefooted donkeys lead Mickey and his friends
up the steep cliffs of the Greek island Santorini.
"I don't think I want to look down," says Minnie.
"I can't wait until we get to the villages on top!"

Daisy rides a camel across the hot sands in the Egyptian desert. Camels don't get thirsty very often, and because their feet have padded bottoms they can walk for miles without stopping.

"This ride is a little bumpy," says Daisy.

"It's not as bumpy as riding in this land buggy!" cries Donald as he bounces by.

In the jungles of India, Mickey and Minnie sit in a
howdah high up on an elephant's back.
"Look at that elephant lift that log!" says Minnie.

"They sure seem used to pushing and pulling heavy loads."

"And to carrying people on their backs, too," adds Mickey.

Big shaggy-haired yaks carry Donald and Daisy up
the steep hills and mountains of Tibet.

"Yaks not only carry people around, but they also
give milk," says Donald.

"I could use a cold glass of yak milk!" says Daisy.

Mickey and Minnie pedal their bicycles down a crowded street in China. Almost everyone gets around China this way because there aren't many cars. Even the taxi Donald and Daisy are riding in is pulled by a bicycle.

The rivers of China are also very crowded. Many different boats travel the waters, including the one that Mickey and Minnie are on, which is called a junk. They sail past ferryboats and past rafts made of bamboo poles.

The quickest way for Mickey and Minnie to cross the miles of flat, open country in Australia is to take a bush plane. Where homes and farms are far apart, doctors use these small propeller planes to visit patients, and mail carriers use them to deliver mail.

Donald travels between the islands in the South Seas in an outrigger canoe. The bamboo outrigger rests on the water on both sides of the canoe to prevent the boat from tipping over.

"Full speed ahead!" cries Donald.

The bullet train in Japan, called a shinkansen, is the fastest train in the world. It can move up to a speed of 149 miles per hour.

"It feels like we're traveling faster than a speeding bullet!" says Daisy.

"That must be how this train got its name," says Minnie.

In Alaska, Mickey and Minnie take a ride on a sled being pulled by eight huskies.

"These dogs go very fast," says Minnie.

"I know," agrees Mickey. "If we want them to go even faster, all we need to do is yell 'Mush!'"

Daisy and Donald ride in an iceboat on the frozen lakes of Canada. The sail catches the wind, and the boat zips along the ice.

"It feels like we're riding on a giant ice skate!" cries Donald.

When it's time to go home, Mickey and his friends go to the airport.

"What a great time we've had!" says Minnie as they head for the plane. "People get around in so many different and exciting ways."

"Yes," says Mickey, smiling. "And there's *one* way to get around we almost forgot—by walking!"

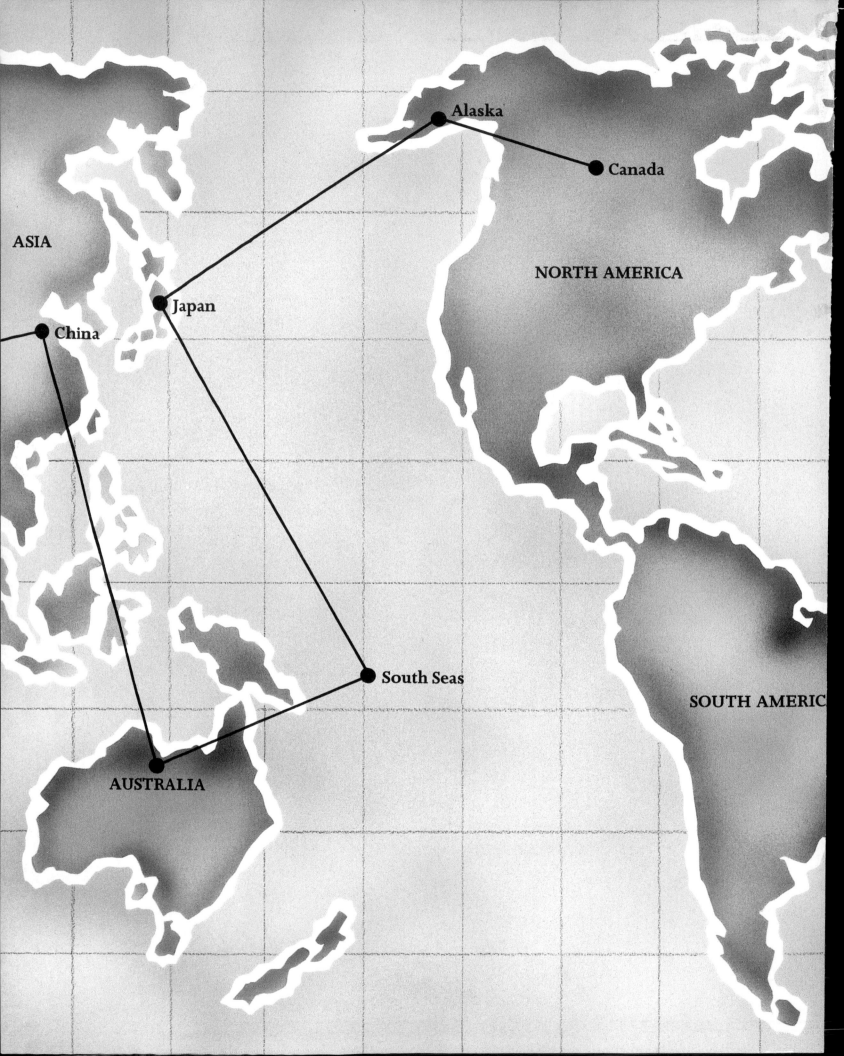